THE SALEM WITCH TRIALS

Robin Johnson

CRABTREE
Publishing Company
www.crabtreebooks.com

Crabtree Publishing Company
www.crabtreebooks.com

Author: Robin Johnson
Publishing plan research and development: Reagan Miller
Editors: Sonya Newland, Kathy Middleton
Proofreader: Wendy Scavuzzo
Photo Researcher: Robin Johnson/ Sonya Newland
Original design: Tim Mayer (Mayer Media)
Book design: Clare Nicholas
Cover design: Ken Wright
Production coordinator and prepress technician: Ken Wright
Print coordinator: Katherine Berti

Produced for Crabtree Publishing Company by White-Thomson Publishing

Photographs:
Alamy: North Wind Picture Archives: pp. 19, 20–21, 38; Everett Collection: p. 37; Bridgeman Art Library: Delaware Art Museum, Wilmington, USA: pp. 34–35; **Corbis:** Bettmann: pp. 12–13, 18, 26, 32–33; Baldwin H. Ward & Kathryn C. Ward: p. 22; Robbie Jack: p. 45; Flickr: David Ohmer: p. 27; Christine Zenino: p. 39; Massachusetts Office of Travel and Tourism: p. 44; **Getty Images:** The Bridgeman Art Library: pp. 14–15; De Agostini: pp. 28–29; **Library of Congress:** pp. 7, 23, 40; Mary Evans Picture Library: p. 9; Everett Collection: pp. 12, 16–17, 41; **Shutterstock:** littleny: pp. 42–43; **SuperStock:** ClassicStock.com: pp. 24–25; **Topfoto:** The Granger Collection: pp. 4–5; **Wikimedia:** cover; pp. 30, 30–31; WILLJAY: pp. 3, 36; Erik K. Smith/Creative Commons Attribution 3.0 License: p. 6; Google Cultural Institution: pp. 10–11.

Library and Archives Canada Cataloguing in Publication

Johnson, Robin (Robin R.), author
The Salem witch trials / Robin Johnson.

(Crabtree chrome)
Includes index.
Issued in print and electronic formats.
ISBN 978-0-7787-1395-1 (bound).--ISBN 978-0-7787-1407-1 (pbk.).--
ISBN 978-1-4271-8983-7 (pdf).--ISBN 978-1-4271-8977-6 (html)

1. Trials (Witchcraft)--Massachusetts--Salem--Juvenile literature.
I. Title. II. Series: Crabtree chrome

KFM2478.8.W5J64 2014 j133.4'3097445 C2014-903924-7
C2014-903925-5

Library of Congress Cataloging-in-Publication Data

Johnson, Robin (Robin R.) author.
The Salem witch trials / Robin Johnson.
p. cm. -- (Crabtree chrome)
Includes index.
ISBN 978-0-7787-1395-1 (reinforced library binding) --
ISBN 978-0-7787-1407-1 (pbk.) --
ISBN 978-1-4271-8983-7 (electronic pdf) --
ISBN 978-1-4271-8977-6 (electronic html)
1. Trials (Witchcraft)--Massachusetts--Salem. 2. Witchcraft--Massachusetts--Salem--History. 3. Salem (Mass.)--History.
I. Title.

KFM2478.8.W5J64 2014
345.744'50288--dc23

2014027806

Crabtree Publishing Company
www.crabtreebooks.com 1-800-387-7650

Printed in Canada/022021/CPC20210129

Published in Canada
Crabtree Publishing
616 Welland Ave.
St. Catharines, ON
L2M 5V6

Published in the United States
Crabtree Publishing
PMB 59051
350 Fifth Avenue, 59th Floor
New York, New York 10118

Published in the United Kingdom
Crabtree Publishing
Maritime House
Basin Road North, Hove
BN41 1WR

Published in Australia
Crabtree Publishing
3 Charles Street
Coburg North
VIC 3058

Contents

Welcome to Salem

▼ *The odd behavior of Betty Parris and Abigail Williams led to some of the strangest and saddest events in American history. This is a fanciful painting of one of the witches in court.*

Strange Days

In 1692, in the village of Salem, Massachusetts, Betty Parris and Abigail Williams began to act very strangely. The two young girls moaned and shrieked. They crawled under tables and tried to climb walls. The girls made strange sounds and saw things that were not there. Their bodies twisted and twitched in unusual ways. They flapped their arms like birds and barked like dogs.

Bewitched!

Betty and Abigail seemed like they were very sick, but they were not. The local doctor could find nothing wrong with them. He saw only one way to explain their odd behavior—the girls were **bewitched**! The doctor's words shocked the good people of Salem and turned their town upside down. This started the biggest—and most deadly—witch hunt in American history.

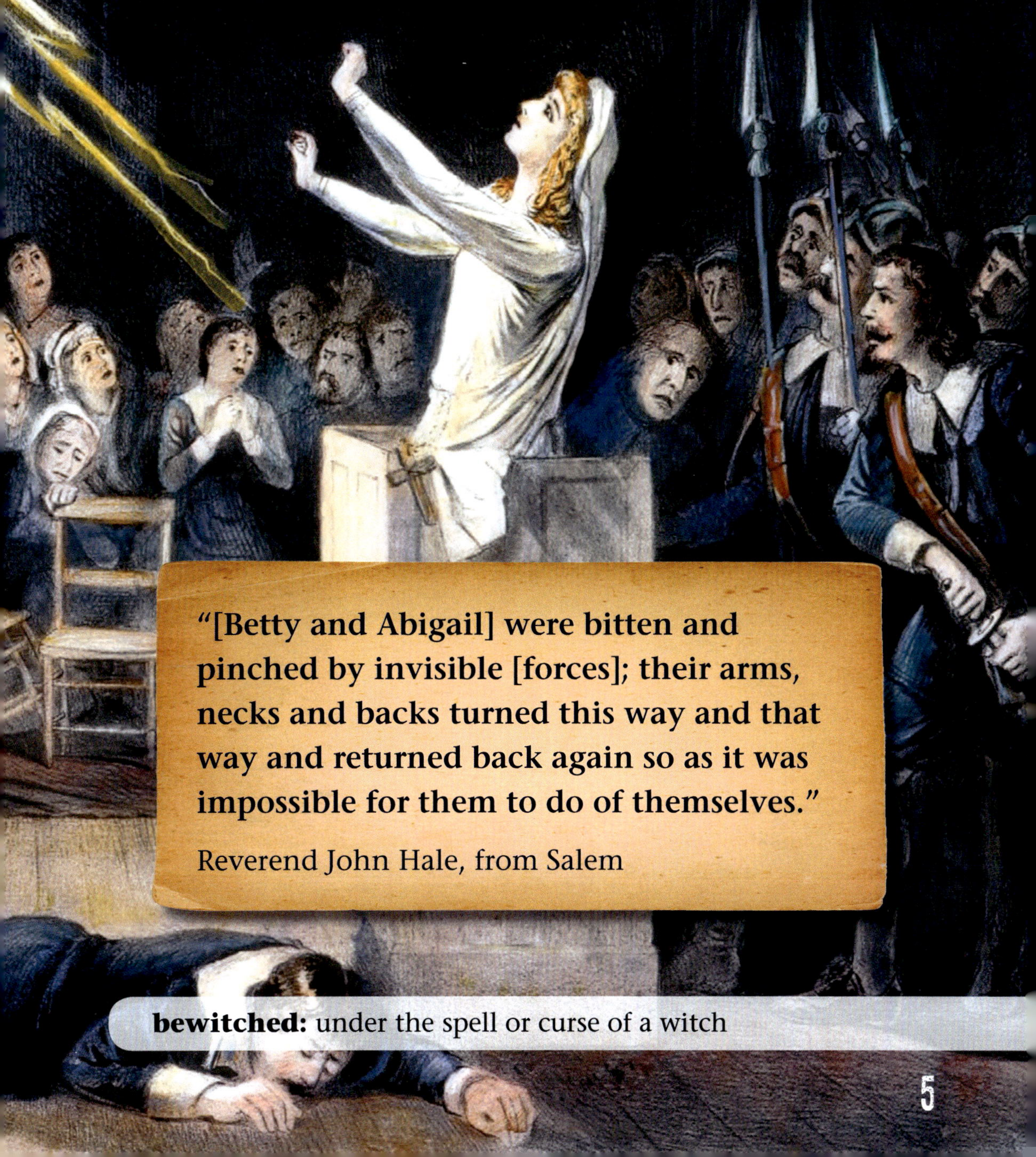

"[Betty and Abigail] were bitten and pinched by invisible [forces]; their arms, necks and backs turned this way and that way and returned back again so as it was impossible for them to do of themselves."

Reverend John Hale, from Salem

bewitched: under the spell or curse of a witch

▲ *This is how Salem Village would have looked when it was first settled in the 1600s. Today, Salem Village is the town of Danvers, Massachusetts. Salem Town is now the city of Salem.*

A Town Divided

In the 1600s, Salem was made up of two areas—Salem Town and Salem Village. Salem Town was a busy coastal town. About 1,500 people lived there. Salem Village was a farming community in the northern part of town. Only about 500 people lived there. The village was growing fast but was always under the control of the larger town.

Growing Tension

As Salem Village grew, many farmers felt it was time for their village to become **independent**. They did not want to be controlled by the wealthy people of Salem Town. They also got tired of having to walk several miles to Salem Town to go to church. Others were happy to stay under Salem Town's rule. The farmers argued fiercely over who should run their growing village.

Salem was founded in 1626 by settlers from Europe. The town got its name—which means "peace"—because the original settlers and the new settlers that moved there worked together to grow the town. Over time, Salem grew less and less peaceful.

▲ *Salem Town was a port town by the sea. The people there fished, built ships, and traded goods.*

independent: free from the control of others

Conflict in the Colonies

Salem was founded during a time when there was great **conflict** between the colonies of North America. The colonies were areas of land settled by Britain, France, and other countries, and ruled over from across the ocean by their kings. Salem was part of a British colony called Massachusetts Bay Colony. British colonies fought French colonies as well as Native American tribes for control of land and the fur trade.

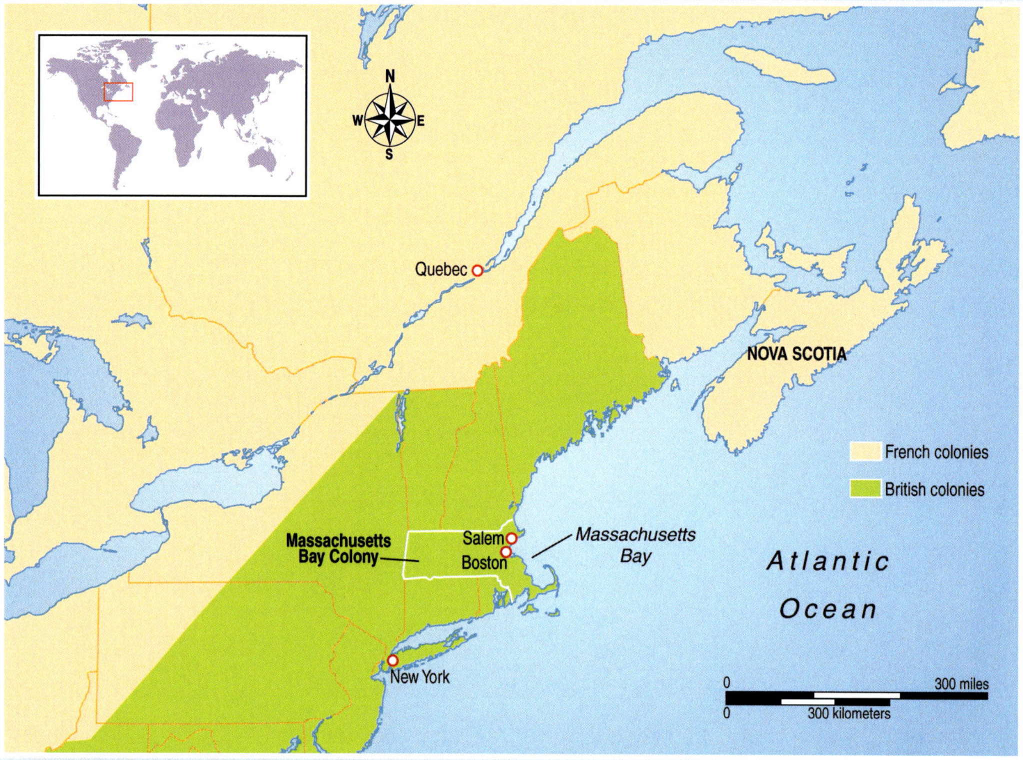

▲ *This map shows the North American colonies in the late 1600s.*

The deeply religious people in Salem Village blamed the devil for the conflict all around them. They believed the devil was a powerful, evil being who fought God for control of their souls.

King William's War

The conflict got worse when King William III of England started a war with France in the colonies in 1689. Most of the fighting took place in what are now Nova Scotia and Quebec in Canada. Many people there left their homes and moved to Salem Village to escape the war. The people of Salem did not trust the newcomers or want to share their success with them.

▲ Frontenac, the governor of the French colonies in North America, refused to surrender to the English during King William's War.

conflict: fighting

Pure and Simple

Most of the people who lived in Salem followed the religion of Puritanism. Puritans were Christians who believed that leading pure, simple lives would bring them closer to God. They worked hard and prayed even harder. Puritans went to church often and did not allow music, dancing, games, or holidays. They wore plain clothes and lived in simple homes.

Puritans lived in England in the 1500s and 1600s. They wanted people there to lead simple, holy lives like they did to get closer to God. They wanted church leaders to dress plainly and give simple services. The English people did not agree with their strict rules and strong beliefs.

The Devil's Work

Most Puritans believed in **witchcraft**. They thought the devil gave people called witches the power to do terrible deeds and harm people, animals, and crops in exchange for their loyalty. They believed that most witches were unfriendly, older women with no children, only pets. Witch hunters looked for signs of the devil on bodies of witches—things such as warts, moles, and birthmarks—to prove they were wicked.

▼ *In 1630, many Puritans left England and settled in Massachusetts so they could practice their religion freely.*

witchcraft: using magical powers to change everyday events

Leading His Flock

In 1689, Salem Village got its own Puritan church. A man named Samuel Parris was chosen to lead the church. Reverend Parris was a stern, serious man. He was also greedy and demanding. Some people tried to force Reverend Parris out of the church, but he would not leave. Instead, he led the charge against evil in Salem Village.

▲ *Reverend Samuel Parris (on the left) warned the villagers of evil. He said, "The devil hath been raised amongst us, and his rage is terrible."*

▶ *The ducking stool was a test to see if someone was a witch. A woman was tied to a chair and dunked in a river. If she floated, she was a witch. If she sank, she was not a witch—but she was dead.*

Looking for Evil

Reverend Parris warned the people of Salem Village that evil was all around them. He said the devil was in their homes and farms, and even in their church! Reverend Parris told the villagers to lead good, Puritan lives and watch for wickedness. The local doctor soon found plenty of it—right in the home of Reverend Parris!

Throughout history, people have blamed magic for things they do not understand. In Europe, tens of thousands of women were killed for practicing witchcraft from the 1300s to the 1600s. In 1641, a law was passed in England that made witchcraft illegal there and in the British colonies.

illegal: against the law

Strange Signs

When Betty Parris and Abigail Williams began to shriek and twitch and show other strange **symptoms**, Reverend Parris called the doctor right away. After all, Betty was his nine-year-old daughter. Abigail was his 11-year-old niece. Dr. William Griggs checked the girls carefully and saw that they were in good health. He concluded that the girls must be "under an evil hand."

Spreading Fast

Soon two more girls began to show the same symptoms as Betty and Abigail. Ann Putnam Jr. and Betty Hubbard were bewitched, too! Ann was the daughter of an important leader in the church. Betty was the niece of the town doctor himself. All four girls came from good Puritan homes in Salem Village. Why would they lie or fake their symptoms?

At the time, doctors did not have formal training. Most of them could read, but there were no medical schools for them to attend. Instead, they learned about sickness and cures by working with other doctors. Only men could be doctors. They often blamed witches—usually women—for illnesses they did not understand.

▼ *The people of Salem Village were scared and confused by the strange symptoms the girls showed.*

symptoms: signs of poor health

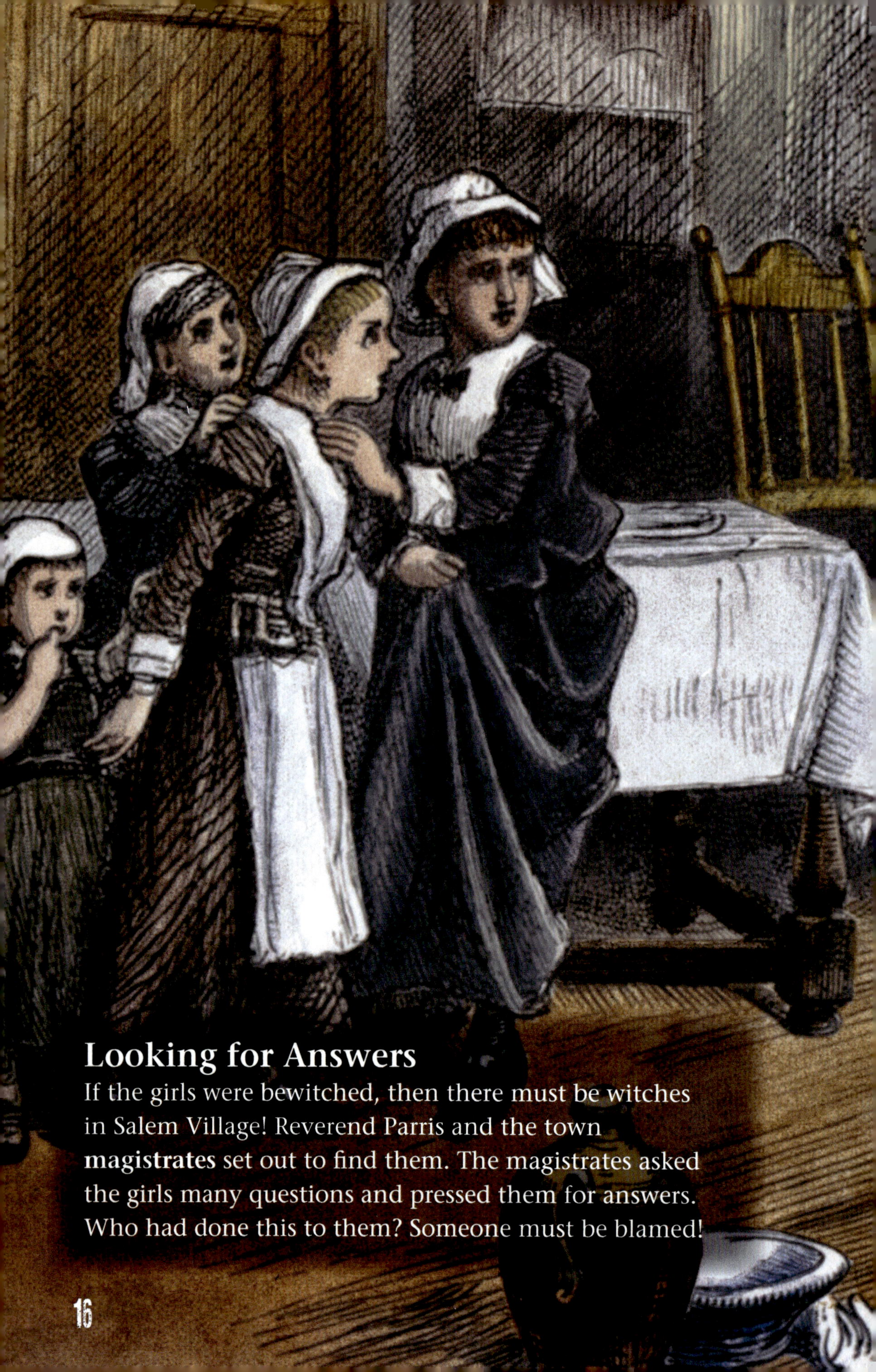

Looking for Answers

If the girls were bewitched, then there must be witches in Salem Village! Reverend Parris and the town **magistrates** set out to find them. The magistrates asked the girls many questions and pressed them for answers. Who had done this to them? Someone must be blamed!

◀ *Tituba's dark skin and colorful stories scared the children of Salem Village.*

Finding Witches

On February 29, 1692, the girls blamed three women for bewitching them. Sarah Good was a homeless beggar who often asked her neighbors for food and shelter. Sarah Osborne was a poor old woman who never went to church. Tituba was an Indian slave owned by Reverend Parris. These women were the first—but not the last—to be blamed for evil in Salem.

People in Salem began using slaves after the Pequot War ended. The Pequot War took place from 1634 to 1638 between the Pequot tribe and British colonists for control of the fur trade. The British won and hundreds of Pequot people were sold into slavery.

magistrates: people who make rules and judge people for crimes

▶ *This woman is being taken to jail for practicing witchcraft. Her hands are open to show she is innocent.*

We Are Not Witches!

On March 1, 1692, the three women were taken to jail. Magistrates spent many days asking them the same questions over and over again. Were they witches? Had they seen the devil? How did they explain the pain they seemed to cause the young girls? Both Sarah Good and Sarah Osborne claimed they were **innocent**. They said they had done nothing wrong.

Tituba's Tales

Tituba, on the other hand, admitted she was a witch! She said that the devil had come to her in the form of a tall man from Boston, a hog, and a great black dog. The devil asked her to sign his book and do his evil work. Tituba also claimed she had flown through the air, riding on poles with Sarah Good, Sarah Osborne, and other witches in town. The people of Salem Village believed Tituba and were eager to catch the other witches.

▲ *Tituba later admitted that Reverend Parris had forced her to lie and say she was a witch.*

"I rid upon a stick or pole and Good and Osborne behind me. We rid taking hold of one another. I don't know how we go for I saw no trees nor path, but was presently there."

Tituba, who claimed to be a witch and helped set the witch hunt in motion

innocent: not guilty of a crime

Not Like the Others

The women first **accused** of witchcraft did not fit in with the other villagers. They were poor. They did not go to church. They looked and acted differently than the Puritan women in Salem Village. It was easy for people to imagine that the devil had gotten to them. But when the girls accused Martha Corey on March 11, 1692, everything changed.

▲ *In court, the girls who accused Martha copied her movements so the jury believed that Martha was controlling them and found her guilty of witchcraft.*

Church Lady

Martha Corey was a good Puritan woman. She went to church often and was well liked in Salem Village. Martha did not believe in witchcraft. She spoke out and said she thought the girls were lying. So they accused her of being a witch! Martha was found guilty as charged and sentenced to death.

"I never had to do with witchcraft since I was born."

Martha Corey

accused: blamed for doing something wrong or bad

Panic Sets In

The villagers were shocked that Martha Corey, a well-respected woman, had been hung for witchcraft. If such a good Puritan woman was a witch, then anyone could be! People began to **panic**. They started looking for witches around every corner. The witch hunt had begun!

▼ *A woman being arrested for witchcraft fights to stay in her home.*

While villagers hunted for witches, families and friends tried to heal the bewitched. They fasted (stopped eating for a period of time). They prayed long and hard for a cure. Betty Parris was sent to live in Salem Town to recover away from the wild witch hunt. Her symptoms soon went away.

The Search Is On

Villagers searched for witches—and found plenty of them. Dozens of women and men were accused of practicing witchcraft. Even several children were accused. Sarah Good's daughter was just four years old when she was arrested and taken to jail. No one was safe in Salem.

▼ *This young Puritan woman looked innocent. Could she be a witch?*

panic: to act wildly after a sudden scare

The Witch Trials

Taken to Town

Accused witches were ripped from their homes and farms, and taken into the village. They were questioned by the magistrates in the village meeting house. Their homes were searched for signs of witchcraft, such as puppets that could be used to cast spells on people. If there was a chance that the accused were witches, they were taken to jail to wait for their **trials**.

▼ *Some accused witches fought and screamed that they were innocent. Others walked calmly to jail and waited for their chance to speak in court.*

After months of witch hunting, the Salem jail was overflowing with prisoners. Some people spent many months in cold, dark, dirty jail cells waiting for their trials. Several prisoners starved to death or caught deadly diseases there.

To Hear and Decide

On May 27, 1692, Governor William Phips formed a special court to judge witchcraft cases. The new court was called the Court of Oyer and Terminer, which means "to hear and decide." Lieutenant Governor William Stoughton was named Chief Justice, or head judge, and put in charge of the court. He had not studied the law and had never heard a court case before.

trials: meetings in court where judges and juries decide cases

The First Case

Bridget Bishop was the first person brought before the new court. She was an older woman who broke all the rules of Puritan society. Bridget drank alcohol, played games, and wore flashy clothes. The judge asked her how she had bewitched the five girls. He demanded to know how she had appeared as a **specter** to her accusers. Bridget denied everything, but it was hopeless. She was found guilty of witchcraft.

▲ *The crowd cheered as Bridget was taken to Gallows Hill and hanged from a tree.*

▲ *Bridget Bishop was the first of many people hanged for witchcraft in Salem.*

A Hopeless Case

For months, a steady stream of accused witches went to court. People who claimed they were innocent were found guilty and hanged. People who confessed were allowed to live, however. The judges thought that witches who confessed were willing to change their evil ways. But many Puritan prisoners refused to lie and say they were witches, even to save their own lives.

"I have done no witchcraft... I am as innocent as the child unborn."

Accused witch, Bridget Bishop

specter: a ghost or spirit

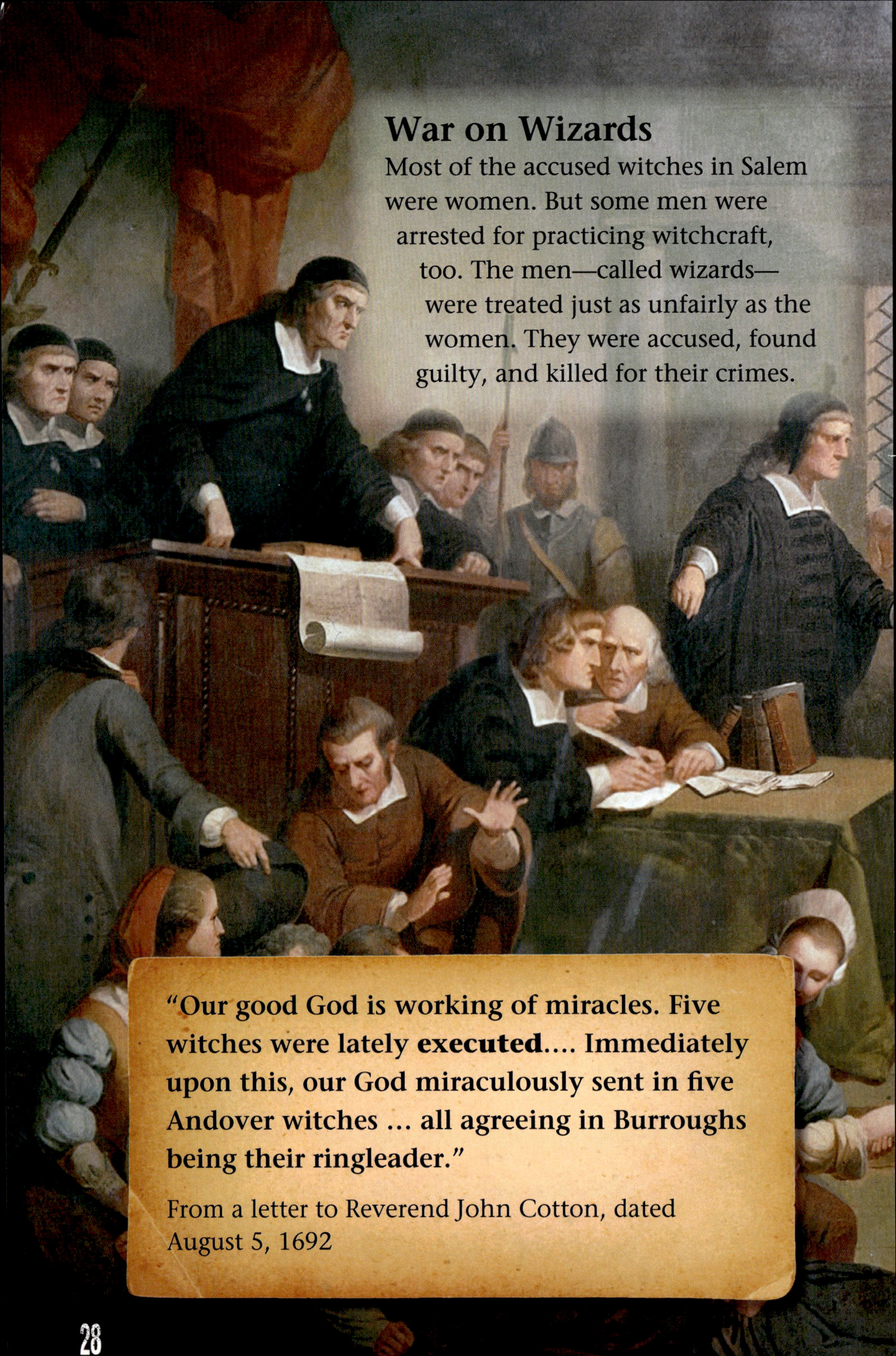

War on Wizards

Most of the accused witches in Salem were women. But some men were arrested for practicing witchcraft, too. The men—called wizards—were treated just as unfairly as the women. They were accused, found guilty, and killed for their crimes.

"Our good God is working of miracles. Five witches were lately executed.... Immediately upon this, our God miraculously sent in five Andover witches ... all agreeing in Burroughs being their ringleader."

From a letter to Reverend John Cotton, dated August 5, 1692

By George

George Jacobs was an old man who was accused by many people—including his own granddaughter. He had a small mark on his shoulder that his accusers called proof he had been touched by the devil. George Burroughs was a minister accused of leading the witches. Even though he repeated the Lord's Prayer perfectly—which Puritans believed witches could not do—he was hanged anyway.

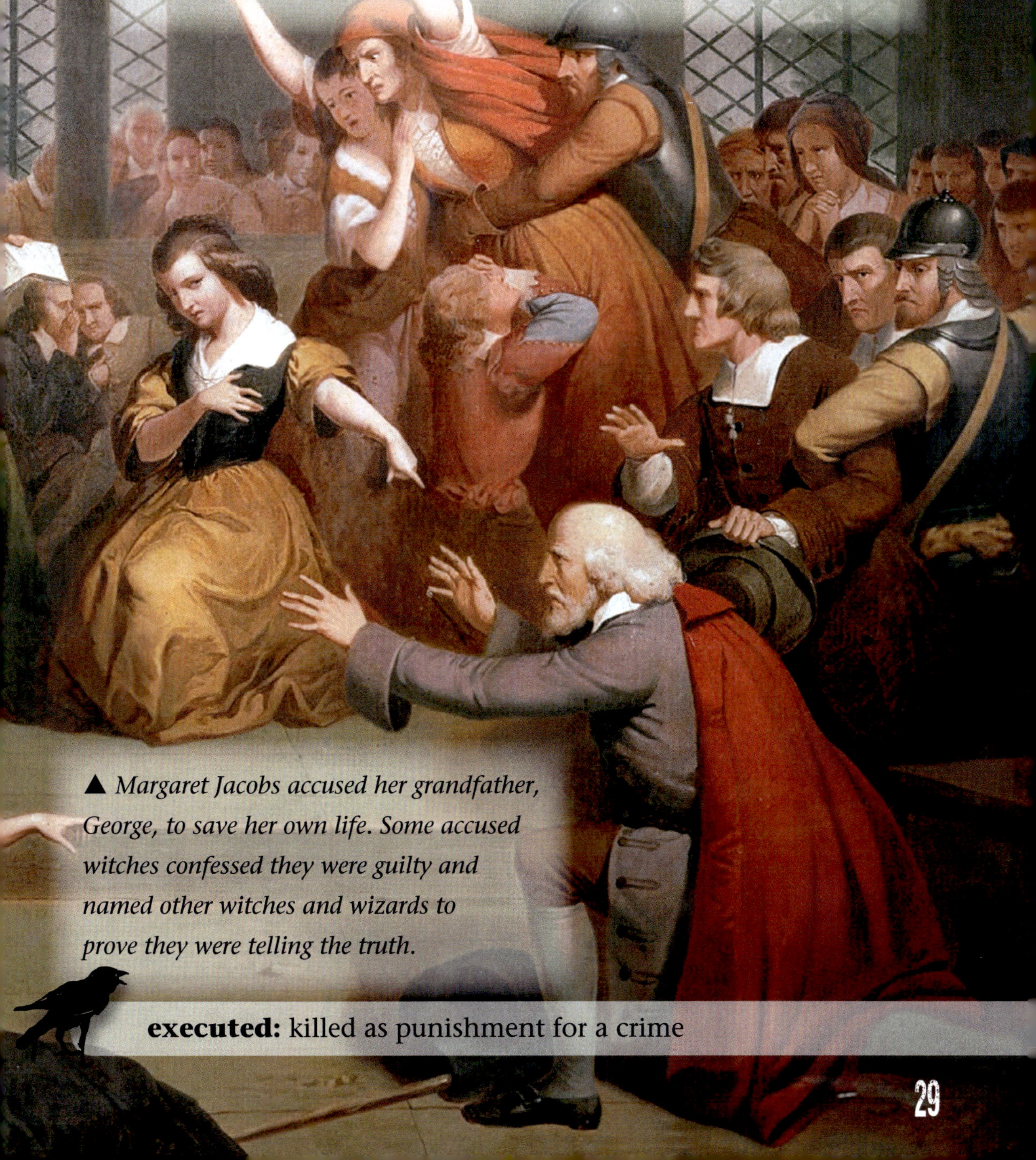

▲ *Margaret Jacobs accused her grandfather, George, to save her own life. Some accused witches confessed they were guilty and named other witches and wizards to prove they were telling the truth.*

executed: killed as punishment for a crime

Pointing the Finger

As the witch trials wore on, more people stepped forward to accuse more witches. Men, women, and children joined the girls who had started the witch hunt. Many accusers came from powerful families. The court did not dare question their stories or disagree with them.

▼ *A witness points to an accused witch during one of the trials in Salem.*

Accused witches were not allowed to use lawyers to help make their cases. They had to defend themselves in court. The witches were guilty until proven innocent. Nearly all the accused swore they were innocent, but the people of Salem wanted them convicted—and the courts did so.

▲ *Marks on the bodies of the accused were pricked with needles. If they did not bleed, or if the accused did not feel the needles, they were believed to be witches.*

Guilty As Charged

Wealthy, powerful people—such as the Putnam and Parris families—ran the village and the courts. They decided which witches should be arrested and what the **verdict** would be. And the verdict was always guilty!

verdict: the decision made by a jury in a trial

Stealing the Show

The accused witches tried hard to make their cases in court. But it was nearly impossible for them to do so. Each day, the court was filled with young women who claimed they were bewitched. They put on a wild show to prove they were telling the truth.

▲ *All sorts of wild behavior was reported in the courtroom. This artist shows books flying around as if a spell had been cast on them.*

Courtroom Circus

The girls screamed in pain when the accused witches talked. They pinched and bit their own arms and poked themselves with pins. The girls fell to the floor and rolled around in **agony**. And they blamed it all on the evil powers of the witches.

"Thorns ... were thrust into their flesh; the accusers were sometimes struck dumb, deaf, blind, and sometimes lay as if they were dead for a while."

A witness account of the Salem Witch Trials

agony: extreme pain

Bad Dreams

The Salem Witch Trials became a nightmare for the accused. Chief Justice Stoughton ruled that dreams and visions could be used as **evidence** in court. Some people said that witches bit or punched or choked them in their dreams. Others claimed to have waking visions of witches doing terrible deeds.

> **"Sarah Good most violently pulled down my head behind a chest and tied my hands together with a wheel band and almost choked me to death, and also several times since the [ghost] of Sarah Good has ... tortured me by biting, pinching, and almost choking me to death."**
>
> 18-year-old accuser, Susanna Sheldon

▲ *When a wolf appeared in Salem in 1692, people believed it must have been bewitched, as wolves had not been seen in those parts for more than 30 years.*

True or False

No one could prove that the dreams and visions were true. However, they were treated as facts in the Salem Witch Trials. In some cases, dreams were the only evidence against accused witches. It was enough proof to send them to their death.

evidence: facts or information used to prove something is true

Innocent!

One person was found innocent in the Salem Witch Trials—but not for long! Rebecca Nurse was a frail old woman who was arrested on March 23, 1692. Rebecca went to church often and was **respected** by most people in the village. However, her family had fought with the powerful Putnam family over land. So the Putnams accused Rebecca of practicing witchcraft.

"I have got nobody to look to but God."

Rebecca Nurse

▼ *This is Rebecca Nurse's homestead in Salem. After Rebecca was hanged for witchcraft, the homestead fell into the hands of the Putnams.*

▲ *Rebecca Nurse is brought in chains to her trial. Rebecca was so respected by the local people that they signed a petition asking that she be freed.*

Think Again!

Throughout her trial, Rebecca swore she was innocent, even though her accusers fell down in fits. But this time, the jury believed the accused! They agreed that Rebecca was not a witch. So Chief Justice Stoughton asked the jury to try again. He sent them out of the court to rethink the verdict. They changed their minds and realized Rebecca was guilty after all.

respected: admired and looked up to for having certain qualities

No Way Out

An accused wizard named Giles Corey saw that there was no way out. His wife Martha had vowed she was innocent and was ordered to be hanged. Giles did not want to confess to being a wizard to save his life. So he said nothing at all. Without a **plea**, his case could not go to trial.

▲ *A woman accused of being a witch pointed the finger at Giles Corey to save her own life. Another girl confirmed that Corey's spirit had visited her and beaten her.*

> **"I ... believe in my heart that Giles Corey is a dreadful wizzard."**
>
> 19-year-old accuser Mercy Lewis on April 19, 1692

▲ *People who were executed as witches or wizards were usually buried quickly in shallow graves. They were not allowed proper Christian burials.*

Pressed to Death

Giles spent five months in jail. Then the magistrates got tired of waiting and tried to force him to make a plea. Giles was placed on his back in the town square. Wooden boards and huge, heavy rocks were put on top of him. He still refused to make a plea. After two days, Giles was crushed to death. His final words were, "More weight."

plea: a formal statement of guilt or innocence

The End Is Near

Case Closed

By the fall of 1692, the witch hunt had gotten wildly out of control, so Governor Phips put an end to it. He stopped the witchcraft arrests. He shut down the Court of Oyer and Terminer and replaced it with another court. The new court did not allow dreams to be used as evidence. The final witch trial took place in May 1693.

▲ *William Phips was the governor of Massachusetts during the period of the Salem Witch Trials.*

"When I put an end to the Court there were at least fifty persons in prison in great misery by reason of the extreme cold and their poverty."

Governor William Phips on February 21, 1693

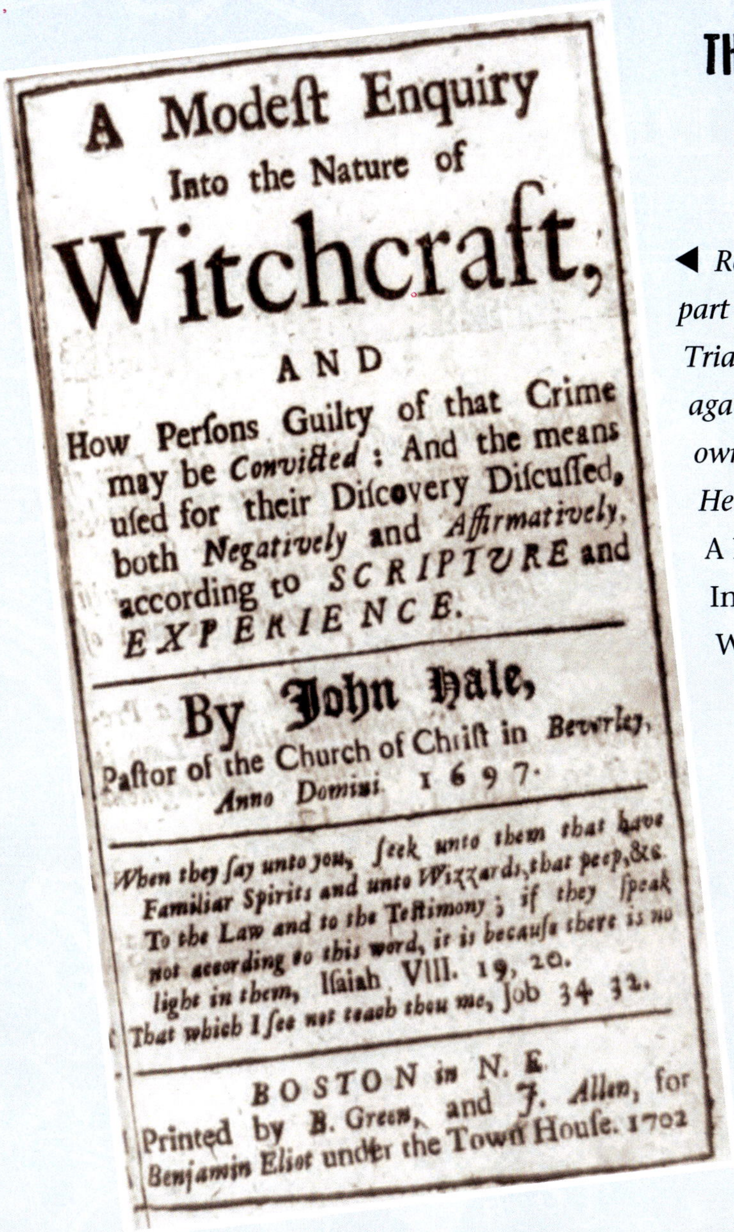

A Modeſt Enquiry
Into the Nature of
Witchcraft,
AND
How Perſons Guilty of that Crime may be *Convicted*: And the means uſed for their Diſcovery Diſcuſſed, both *Negatively* and *Affirmatively*, according to *SCRIPTURE* and *EXPERIENCE*.

By John Hale,
Paſtor of the Church of Chriſt in *Beverley*,
Anno Domini 1697.

When they ſay unto you, ſeek unto them that have Familiar Spirits and unto Wizzards, that peep, &c. *To the Law and to the Teſtimony; if they ſpeak not according to this word, it is becauſe there is no light in them*, Iſaiah VIII. 19, 20.
That which I ſee not teach thou me, Job 34 32.

BOSTON in N. E.
Printed by *B. Green*, and *J. Allen*, for *Benjamin Eliot* under the Town Houſe. 1702

◀ *Reverend John Hale took part in the Salem Witch Trials, but then spoke out against them when his own wife was accused. He wrote a book called* A Modest Enquiry Into the Nature of Witchcraft.

Pardon Me

Governor Phips **pardoned** the prisoners who were still in jail. They were allowed to go free—once they had paid for the food they had eaten there! Some prisoners spent their life savings to get out of jail. They returned to their farms and found that their crops had died while they were locked up. Others could not afford to ever get out of prison.

pardoned: forgiven for a crime and allowed to go free

The Death Toll

The Salem Witch Trials lasted for more than a year. During that time, 200 people were accused of practicing witchcraft. The **death toll** included 19 people who were hanged at Gallows Hill. One man was pressed to death. Several people died in prison waiting for their trials. Two dogs were killed for working with witches!

Forgive Us

Many villagers apologized for what they had said and done during the witch trials. Some even confessed that they had lied in court! The villagers begged God and the families they hurt to forgive them. Ann Putnam Jr. was the only young girl who said she was sorry, however. Years after the trials ended, Ann claimed that the devil had tricked her into lying.

In 1711, the Government of Massachusetts passed a bill that gave the victims back their rights and good names. It also gave the families some money to help pay for their losses. In 1957, Massachusetts finally apologized to the victims of the Salem Witch Trials.

◀ *The home of one of the magistrates in the trials—Judge Jonathan Corwin—still stands in Salem. It is known as the "Witch House."*

death toll: the number of deaths from an action or event

Still Hunting

The Salem Witch Trials took place more than 300 years ago. No one has been executed for witchcraft in the United States since then. But people are still interested in Salem's dark history and visit the town to tour the historic sites. Today, the term "witch hunt" is used when people find and hurt others who are different or who have unpopular views.

▲ *Today, the Salem Witch Museum is a popular tourist attraction.*

▲ *The story of Salem has captured people's imaginations for centuries. This is a scene from a play by Arthur Miller about the witch trials, called* The Crucible.

Witchcraft Today

Today, people around the world practice witchcraft. They use herbs, potions, and **rituals** to contact spirits, cure illnesses, and do other types of supernatural acts. For example, Wicca is a modern religion in which witches worship the earth and nature. The witches do not believe in the devil. They promise to do no harm with their magic.

Some people believe that a fungus in the rye bread the girls ate made them sick. Others think the girls faked the whole thing because they were bored in their small, strict Puritan village. What do you think?

rituals: a series of actions that form a special ceremony

Learning More

Books

Salem Witch Trials: Colonial Life
by Sean Price (Raintree Fusion, 2008)

The Salem Witch Trials: An Unsolved Mystery from History
by Jane Yolen and Heidi E.Y. Stemple (Simon and Schuster, 2004)

The Salem Witch Trials (Graphic History)
by Michael Martin (Graphic Library, 2005)

Who Were the Accused Witches of Salem?: And Other Questions About the Witchcraft Trials (Six Questions of American History)
by Laura Hamilton Waxman (Lerner Publishing Group, 2012)

You Wouldn't Want to Be a Salem Witch!: Bizarre Accusations You'd Rather Not Face
by Jim Pipe (Franklin Watts, 2009)

Websites

http://salem.lib.virginia.edu/home.html
Salem Witch Trials: Documentary Archive and Transcription Project

http://law2.umkc.edu/faculty/projects/ftrials/salem/salem.htm
Famous American Trials: Salem Witchcraft Trials 1692

www.smithsonianmag.com/history/a-brief-history-of-the-salem-witch-trials-175162489/?no-ist
Smithsonian: A Brief History of the Salem Witch Trials

www.nationalgeographic.com/features/97/salem/
National Geographic: Interactive Witch Trials

www.salemwitchmuseum.com/education/index.php
Salem Witch Museum: The Salem Witch Trials of 1692

Glossary

accused Blamed for doing something wrong or bad

agony Extreme pain

bewitched Under the spell or curse of a witch

conflict Fighting

death toll The number of deaths from an action or event

evidence Facts or information used to prove something is true

executed Killed as punishment for a crime

illegal Against the law

independent Free from the control of others

innocent Not guilty of a crime

magistrates People who make rules and judge people for crimes

panic To act wildly after a sudden scare

pardoned Forgave someone for a crime and allowed them to go free

plea A formal statement of guilt or innocence

respected Admired and looked up to for having certain qualities

rituals A series of actions that form a special ceremony

specter A ghost or spirit

symptoms Signs of poor health

trials Meetings in court where judges and juries decide cases

verdict The decision made by a jury in a trial

witchcraft Using magical powers to change everyday events

Index

Entries in **bold** refer to pictures